BROOKLYN NIGHT

I survived!

A mothers birthing story!

First edition

This book was professionally typeset on Reedsy.
Find out more at reedsy.com

Contents

1

Introduction

This is my story of an ordinary woman like yourself becoming a Mother! I had absolutely no idea what to expect or feel, so by reading this if you're pregnant maybe it will show you that every story is different and to try to enjoy every moment you can. It may not always be rainbows and butterflies but it's definitely worth it all. Through the tears, the gray hairs, the scare's,and the scars, the stress, the breakdowns and the laughs, every single moment is worth it.

And believe me it goes by so fast, at first their babies, drinking nothing but milk, soon enough they're eating a lil bit of food and crawling. Next thing you know they're off and running into everything in sight. Then they're talking and know it all, but they still need mama. Soon that fades and they're pushing you away trying to be cool for the girls. Mudding up trucks and going on dates, graduating, getting married and having babies, and living their lives. It goes by so fast, in just a blink of an eye!

2

Chapter 2

I had no idea the amount of love you could feel for another creature, a creature you carried in your womb, a creature who just wrecks your body, a creature that pushes you to your utmost limits. The Love though, the love is like absolutely nothing in this world.

My journey didn't really start when I became pregnant more so when Lil William the third came roaring into this world Christmas morning of 2016. I had never wanted children and was absolutely terrified of being a bad or disappointing parent. I stood in the bathroom of our tiny house and stared at the pregnancy test as a plus sign slowly appeared. My hubby came in from behind me to see what I was doing and got a big grin on his face. "We're having a baby!" He exclaimed, he was happy, I was terrified.

At the time my hubby and I had been married for about 3 years, we were not the best with money, and currently living rent free on my parents ranch in the guest house and still had no money saved. A small one bedroom one bath cottage type, so when we became pregnant we needed to start looking for a house. We were still in debt due to our spending habits and now needed money for a house payment and everything that comes with babies. Money is always an issue, it seems.

We knew roughly what we wanted in a house and how much we wanted our mortgage to not go over. Finding a house was a rough adventure, so many things I would have done differently. Most importantly find a good banker and a good realter that work together well. We started looking and luckily for us the market was low so prices weren't sorring yet. We wanted some land and to not be so super close to any neighbors, we wanted three to four bedrooms and possibly two bathrooms. Turns out that is a lot to ask for on a small budget, every house was either a great house and shop on 0 land or land and horrible house. And of course you can only look for the ones that you can get with your loan type, so the house hunt continued on through both my pregnancies.

My pregnancy wasn't exactly roses but for the most part not terrible, until the time came for baby to change positions. He decided to roll the wrong way and lodged his lil head under my left rib, which sticks out quite noticeably then the right one. Thank you very much son LOL. The things our bodies go through to have a baby is just incredible, and the forever changes to them since having them, that we have to live with every day is also incredible.

However it still wasn't a bad or horribly hard pregnancy, his birth was a slightly different story. Christmas morning around 10am I had just finished showering, and was resting on the bed for a minute while rubbing lotion on my growing belly, before the trek of getting dressed began. I was 35 weeks exactly. I started feeling this odd leaking sensation coming from my who ha, when suddenly water flooded the bed. My husband looked at me white as a ghost and mutters "Love, I think your water just broke." And just like that, at lightning speed the man was dressed, throwing my clothes at me, and started the car before I had lifted myself off the bed! I had never seen him move so fast in my life! LOL

I slowly got up and walked to the bathroom wondering if I had just peed or something crazy, I was in complete denial, thinking to myself "not on Christmas". I didn't feel different, nothing was happening other than the water seemed to just not stop trickling out of me after the great flood had happened on my bed. Completely unsure of what to do about the water still dripping out of me I throw a pad on and manage to get dressed and my hubby helps me into the car.

Meanwhile outside it's snowing like it did in 66, and we live out on a three mile dirt road in the middle of nowhere, and then another 20 miles to our local hospital. It's a minimum of 30 minutes to the hospital on a clear day. We start the trek out the drive and we come to our first fallen tree on the dirt road. In the middle of the mad panic as we were first time parents and five weeks ahead of schedule, we were not prepared to be doing this on this stormy Christmas morning. My hubby needed to grab the saw so throwing the car in reverse we start to get stuck and he decides to just get out and run to the house and get the saw. And right about now is when the labor pains start kicking in and the contractions are not far apart. I know my baby is breached and I know I need to have a Cesarean so I begin to worry that depending on how many trees are down we may not make it to the hospital before he comes.

My hubby gets the tree down and off we go, three more trees cut and we hit pavement and I'm in full out contractions every three minutes! The pavement was slick and icy due to the Christmas storm we were having but my hubby did amazing driving as fast as he safely could. Any other time I would have loved the Christmas snow, but not today, today it was a scary obstacle on our way to the hospital.

3

Chapter 3

We arrived at the hospital in absolute record time, considering, and alive! We go in and let the nurses know what is happening, they jump into action and start the process of having me sign fifty papers all while sticking needles in me multiple times because my veins are being hard to find, it took the nurse three times to put in the IV. "Ouch."

The nurse let me know that they were still trying to reach a Doctor, any Doctor, but so far no luck. After more time passes they start to spitball about sending me in an ambulance to Eugene which is just over an hour away. However my contractions and dilation said I would not make it to the other hospital. I was terrified!

The clock was ticking and we were going to have to make a decision soon, we were either going to have to try the ambulance or an on-call Doctor would possibly answer the phone on Christmas morning.

Finally Dr Anderson answers the on call phone and comes in, now the only wait is the anesthesiologist. Tick tock tick tock. All I could think was it's definitely too late to try for the other hospital now, but what happens if the anesthesiologist doesn't come? I had never been so scared in my entire life, not for myself but for my son's life, I knew for him I

5

could endure anything I needed to to save him.

The minutes passed and every contraction hit like a butter knife to my insides, the Doctors started to discuss options in the event the anesthesiologist did not answer. A nurse ran down the hall to the Doctors outside my door and said "she will be here in five minutes!" Dr Anderson walked in and informed me it was time to proceed and they were going to go scrub up and would see me in the OR shortly.

A few minutes later they got me into the OR, moved me to the operating bed, leaned me up and as I contracted they shoved a needle in my spine, laid me back down and pulled a cover in front of me just under my breasts, so I could not watch and my hubby could not watch them open me up.

As the pain disappeared and I relaxed, the only thought that came to mind was I'm finally going to meet my son, am I going to be a good mother? Please let me be able to be what he needs!

They let my hubby in to sit by my side and hold my hand. The Doctor soon said " Ok you're gonna feel pressure on your chest like an elephant is sitting on you, we are gonna push him out, a minute later there he was, 5lbs 11oz, 23 inches long. I had never seen anything so absolutely perfect, he was so tiny and handsome, he was everything I could have ever dreamed of. They did a quick clean up and made sure he was ok before bundling him up and laying on my chest so I could hold him.

My hubby and I stared at this beautiful lil wonder we had created with our love. He had amazing bright blue eyes and a full head of shaggy black hair, (that later fell out and grew back bleach blonde with a cute lil dark spot of hair just above his left ear where his head was stuck under my left rib).

That first night in the hospital was just tiring, my lil man was in a lil bassinet and my hubby was asleep on the couch like thing that was in my recovery room. Lil man would cry every few hours for milk or a butt change, I hated that I could not move and get up to take care of him. I was literally stuck in bed, my legs were like jelly, there was no getting up yet.

I remember lil man waking up crying and I tried to wake my hubby and he literally slept through lil man's cries and my hallering until finally a nurse came in and asked me if I needed some help. I laughed awkwardly and nodded, she told me to just buzz her anytime lil man woke up and she would come in and feed him and change him. I answered, "Can I feed him?" She smiled and nodded.

The next morning they removed my catheter and wanted me to get up and take a shower. It had been 24 hours since my cesarean, standing up for the first time had to be the most painful thing I had ever experienced. My legs didn't quite feel like they were attached exactly. The slicing pain I felt through my abdomen was unreal, it truly changed the way I perceived pain.

From then on I had to get up to use the restroom and so I honestly didn't want to drink very much, which did not help the insane constipation I ended up having.

December 27th, we went home two days after giving birth, which looking back is a lil early for a cesarean but that's our local Hospital for you. However me and the baby were fine, we went home and became accustomed to being parents of a newborn. It was hard for a bit while I healed up, but with help from my hubby, when he came home from work and help from my mom for a few days I was able to sleep and heal.

I remember in our old house the toilet seat was always freezing, and I mean freezing! The first thing my hubby did after he got me settled on the couch and lil man by my side, he slipped socks on the toilet seat, so it would be warmer for me when I sat down on it. I don't know where he came up with the idea but it worked, it stopped me from jerking up from the cold toilet seat and hurting myself. It was the sweetest thing in the whole world to me!!

My milk had yet to come in so we were pumping and taking every possible supplement and herb possible to get it to kick in, but it just was not happening. After two weeks we gave up and had to rely solely on formulas, which worked fine at first. When lil Willaim was about eight weeks old he started to develop what we know now as a milk protein allergy, but at the time my lil man just started throwing up after every bottle, and I had no idea why. Looking back, being a parent is just one learning event after another, we honestly have no idea what we are doin, just trying to do the best that we can.

I took him multiple times to the pediatrician to be told to just try different formulas. Looking back I would have changed Doctors after this, but hind sight and all that. Four weeks went by still with no change, lil William is 12 weeks old and not holding down food.

Each time I would get my hopes up that this formula was it, this one would be the right one and I wouldn't have to see my lil man throw up after every bottle and have his Doctor say well he's not losing weight so just keep trying different formulas for at least 2 weeks before trying another. Lil man never made it past day nine.

This is also the time I have my 12 week check up with my OBGYN. My Doctor came into the room and informed me that my urine came back positive on the pregnancy test! "What now?" I sputtered "We have only made love once! Maybe twice?" She laughed and said that's all it takes!

So sure enough with a 12 week old baby who was yet to hold down a bottle and I still had 0 idea as to why. I was now pregnant with number two, my Doctor warned me that this pregnancy would likely be more painful then the first due to the fact that I had just been cut in half 12 weeks earlier and my body was still healing. And it would also be likely that baby number two would also come early.

Let me tell you she was not fibbing about there being more pain then the first, as my hips moved and my body tried to heal as well as make room for another nugget it was unpleasant to say the least. She also warned me that I really needed to not gain more than 15 pounds with this baby because the added pressure to the fusing scar could cause more complications.

Let me tell you, craving control was sooo very hard. I love milk, however I'm Lactose intolerant, and if I drank milk it would make me sick. So I couldn't have the main thing I craved which was milk!

$$4$$

Chapter 4

Weeks start to go by balancing work, marriage, parenthood to a baby who can't seem to hold down formula of any kind, and being pregnant with a body that was still healing from the first go.

Finally when lil William was about six months old a friend suggested Alimentum by Similac, that her son had had similar problems and this formula had helped him. I ran to the store and bought some, at first with the powder mix there was no change, so she suggested the premix liquid kind instead of the powder.

I tried this and finally after four months of trying almost every kind of formula out there and getting no help from my pediatrician lil William made it past nine days. After we switched he was finally able to hold down a bottle.

Around this same time I was four months pregnant with number two, and it was time for an ultrasound. I was super excited about this visit because this was the same visit I had when I found out lil William was a boy, and well I was hoping today she would be able to tell me the same.

William and I had always talked about having two boys together, if I ever had the nerve to become a parent with him. We had even picked out their names previously to ever conceiving, he wanted our first son to be named after him which would make him lil William the third. I wanted our second son to be named after my brother who had passed away when we were kids and a middle name after my fathers first.

So needless to say with already having one boy I had my fingers crossed that this one would be as well. At first the baby was being tricky and it was hard for her to be certain of the sex, and she didnt want to say right off, but eventually she smiled and said "Its a boy!!" I smiled, staring at the tiny blob on the screen and said, "Hello Matthew Daniel!" I was over the moon.

5

Chapter 5

Soon after the discovery of Matthew's gender, we found a house we decided to buy.

It was a cute three bedroom one bath house on an acre. It was an older house that needed work, a lot ish of work but we got it for $150,000. Before we moved in we had to replace ALL the flooring. We don't exactly know what's under our carpet, because we had the Lowe's guys come and rip out the old Orange shag carpet that stretched through the house, and replaced it with Beautiful super soft super blush carpet. We charged it on our credit card and went overboard because our last house had had horrible super thin outside carpet for inside carpet that was laid over concrete with no padding. So ya we went all out on the carpet in the living room and the bedrooms.

We also had to tear out the kitchen and the flooring and by tear out the kitchen I mean tear out the cabinets and the walls down to the studs. We learned quickly that our 1940s house was made of cinder block, then 1x1's, then 1x12's nailed onto those, then wallpaper on top of the 1x12's. The cabinets and countertops were rotten, so was the wall behind the kitchen sink. The kitchen was so small we tore out a wall to open it up into the living room to expand it with an open Island. Which we did all ourselve!

We charged new beautiful oak cabinets and nice laminate countertops. The floor was so uneven in the kitchen it dropped four inches from the front to the back. I suggested saving money and the headache of figuring out how to lay a proper floor on a very uneven multi-layered surface and just get a nice looking linoleum that was easy to lay. We had unearthed 4 different layers of flooring in the kitchen before we decided to stop.

Months passed uncomfortably as we were in the middle of a large remodel in our new home. We had the kitchen and dining room completely gutted down to the bones, we had the living room gated off so lil man couldn't go crawling into the war zone. We were living out of a microwave and a fridge, and take out!

My body seemed to ache constantly, my hips hurt, my back hurt, my breasts hurt, my pelvic bones and incision hurt! Everything hurt! Taking care of Lil William was becoming increasingly harder as he and I both grew.

We were coming up on his first birthday/ Christmas (insert eye roll here, I still can't believe he decided to come on Christmas morning, ugh we now refer to it as "Birthmas") and my 35 week check up.

December 20th, the morning of my check up, I had gained a total of thirteen pounds so far. My Doctor checked my dilation and told me I was dilated to 2 cm which was normal for 35 weeks. When she checked me there was no pain or anything abnormal. She informed me that since William had come at 35 weeks we should start to prepare ourselves, that he could potentially come any time. She told me I should roughly be in the safe zone if I happen to go into labor before my due date, and that my baby should not need to be taken to the pediatric hospital in Eugene.

I laughed and told her I had prepared for his arrival over the weekend, I had set his bassinet up and installed the car seat, I even got all his clothes and diapers set up and put in his dresser. Lil Man was also still in diapers at not even a year old yet.

The next morning around 6am on the morning of December 21st 2017 my hubby and I made love and sure enough, true to myth it may or may not have kicked me into labor. Just after we finished I started having contractions, we started talking about my hubby staying home from work until they stop just in case they dont he would be able to take me to the hospital.

An hour passes and my contractions continue and become closer and closer together, roughly three minutes apart. He lets his employer know he is not coming to work but rather taking me to the hospital. We got a hold of my mother to meet us at the hospital to take my 4 days away from becoming a one year old son Lil William.

We get to the hospital around 8am, my mother takes Lil William and my hubby and I go into the delivery wing. The nurses start the process of hooking me up to monitor me and the baby and my contractions. Two hours pass and my contractions are less than three minutes apart for over 45 minutes, the nurse checks my dilation and I let out a scream!

The day before when my Dr had done it there was 0 pain, this morning however it was life the nurse stabbed my uterus. My reaction starttled the nurse and I explained that it had hurt like hell. So she grabs the head nurse and she now wants to check me, again I yelp out in pain it felt as though she had stabbed me with a dull blade. The nurses consulted each other and informed me my Doctor would be in shortly to check me. Minutes or so later my Doctor came into the room and wanted to check my dilation, I was not happy knowing it was probably going to hurt badly again!

She came into the room and laughed at me and said "When I told you , you were in the safe zone I didn't mean for you to go ahead and go into labor!"

She came over to check my dilation and sure enough she checked me and this time my body bucked and I yelped, she looked up at me frowning and informed me we were going to go ahead and do a c section right now. She let the nurses know and they started the process of preparing me for the Operating Room. At this point I'm unsure of what is goin on other than that it had hurt like hell, and something seemed to be wrong.! However I was hopeful because William had been born at 35 weeks and was perfectly fine.

I was roughly familiar with the next steps of heading into the Operating Room and them shoving the needle into my spine and laying down while they washed my body with antibacterial soaps. However this time I very much felt the nurse press her finger into my belly button which had yet to pop out, and it felt very uncomfortable to say the least. I let out an "Ow" and the anesthesiologist asked me if I could feel that and I nodded yes.

They leaned me back more on my head to help the blood push the numbing medicine through my body, after a min I can still feel it and she warns she might have to put me under if it doesn't kick in, moments later it blissfully did and for a bit the pain was gone. They asked one more time if I could feel anything. I said no and heard the chilling words "Ok, good im making my first incision."

They then let my hubby into the room to be by my side as we were about to welcome our second son into the world. Moments later I felt the elephant pressure on my chest which queued them pulling him out, and there he was lil Matthew Danial, 5 lbs 7 ozs 23" long, he was just as perfect as our first son. Long shaggy black hair and bright blue eyes!!

They put him on my chest for a few moments to see and hold him, then it was time for my hubby and Matthew to be taken out while they stitched me up. This time four layers of staples and three layers of stitches to help keep me closed since this was a back to back Cesarean.

6

Chapter 6

I'm moved to my recovery room, where I get to see Matthew and my hubby. I watched as they bathed, weighed and measured him. I get to hold him for another few minutes before she wants to take him so they can check my incision and vitals.

The nurse comes in and informs me Matthew is having trouble breathing, and is having the pediatric nurse check him out. I'm still coming down from the strong numbing medicine and quickly ask what she means. Before she could answer, the head pediatric nurse tells us that Matthew seems to continue to stop breathing for a few seconds then takes a breath. She fears at 35 weeks his lungs were not ready for the world.

She informs me that she may have to make the decision to send him to Riverbend, the closest Pediatric hospital to us where he would be properly taken care of until he could breath on his own.

Matthew ultimately made the decision for us as his gaps in breath continued to grow, she made the call and Riverbend sent an ambulance down to take him away. My heart broke when they then informed me that I would have to remain at Mercy since I had just had major surgery.

When the ambulance arrived, they took Matthew into another room and put him in a special box with breathing support and IV's, when I saw him next, tears slid from my eyes. They wheeled him into the room in this large cube like box that was clear, so you could see in. He was so tiny, so very tiny. He was hooked up to wires and IV's and had a breathing apparatus over his tiny face. I thought I was going to die inside.

They opened up a side panel so I could reach over and touch him one more time before they took him away. I rubbed his tiny foot and worked so hard not to start sobbing but I couldn't stop the tears from streaming down my face.

The nurses said "Alright Mama, time to say goodbye!" They closed the hatch and wheeled him out of the room. My hubby kissed my forehead and said he would call when he was up there and settled in with him, and quickly left to catch up with the ambulance and his mom who had just arrived and was going to accompany him to Riverbend.

The minute they were gone I fell apart sobbing, completely emotional. They had just taken my newborn son from me, I was a complete wreck with hard uncontrollable emotional sobs. Soon enough the tears of a broken heart quickly turned to tears of pain. The body sobbing started to pull and tear at my stitches and staples as the numbing wore off and pain was quickly all I could think about.

For anyone who has cried or laughed or even coughed hard for any amount of time knows it takes abdominals to do so and they had just cut through 7 layers of mine.They upped my pain meds a touch but it didn't seem to do anything, I soon started sobbing from the pain which only made it intensify more and that made me sob harder. It felt like I was tearing apart.

I remember my mother looking at me and stomping out of my room and hollering at the nurses. "Hello can we get some help in here!" and then "My daughter is in real pain and nothing has helped her so far, there has to be something you can give her!" Shortly after the nurses got a hold of my Doctor and let her know the situation, she prescribed a shot of something I'm assuming morphine of some kind.The nurse injected it into and after a full hour I finally felt the pain start to subside, and I could breathe again.

I had to work over time to not start crying when the phone rang just after the drugs kicked in. It was my hubby video calling me so I could see my son. I let the tears fall staring at him through the tiny screen, he was hooked up to so many different things. It broke my heart to see his tiny body in that plastic box, with all those wires and cords.

My sister in law soon brought Lil William in to see me and snuggle for a bit before my mother took him home to her house. While I stayed in the hospital to recover and William was up at Riverbend with Matthew my mom was going to watch lil William for us.

When it was time for my mom and lil Willaim to leave and get settled at her house, again I had to hold my sobs in knowing that if I couldn't it would tear me up more. This was the first time I was ever apart from lil William overnight. Yes I was that mom and super overprotective of my lil nugget and had never let anyone watch him for a night yet. I hugged my lil man with all my heart and soul and wished him sweet dreams.

My sister n law then stayed with me until midnight, not leaving me alone even though she had work early in the morning. Her staying with me those next hours and just talking about nothing to distract me, meant so very much to me.

Those of us who have had babies know what a crazy emotional roller coaster you are after giving birth. Midnight came and she wished me well and headed home, I layed there for what seemed like forever trying to sleep. Anyone who has spent any time in a hospital knows, they do not let you sleep because they have to check on you every hour or two. So rest or sleep is truly impossible.

The night crawled by as I layed there missing my babies and husband, William video chatted me so I could see my newborn and him, he couldn't sleep or rest at Riverbend either. I had to stay at Mercy from Thursday through to Saturday morning when I was released which is crazy for a c section but that's our hospital for ya.

That first night I woke up to pain and felt myself gushing blood from between my legs. I called for the nurses and they helped me slowly stand to change my dressing and the bedding. The nurse says that's pretty common to expel blood clots especially since I had sobbed so hard right after surgery.

The next day Friday December 22nd they asked me if I wanted to be released so I could go see Matthew? I say yes of course but my body was not done expelling blood clots and the Doctor says I have to stay another night. Looking back I'm floored that the hospital would even offer me a discharge after having a cesarean 24 hours before!

Saturday morning finally arrives and they discharge me! My mother leaves Lil William with my sister n law to watch and pick me up from the hospital. She takes me home to shower and get clothes then drives me to Eugene where Matthew and my hubby are.

7

Chapter 7

It was in the middle of flu season so my mother was not allowed into the pediatric wing, so my hubby met us down at the entrance with a wheelchair. I say my goodbyes to my mother, and she heads home to pick up and take care of Lil William for however long I was gonna be in Eugene.

My hubby first wheels me to the room the hospital had graciously lent us since our baby was there and they were not near capacity. He helped me use the bathroom and drop off my bags in the room.

Next we wheel to the pediatric wing, we scrub up and get ringed in, he wheels me to the last room on the left where my baby boys awaits. The nurses look up at me and asked " Are you mom?", I nodded unable to take my eyes off my tiny 5lb 7oz baby boy, hooked up to all shorts of machines including a breathing apparatus, a Iv in his tiny leg and a feeding tube going in his nose and down his throat.

My heart broke.

The nurse tells me to take off my shirt, that I needed to do skin to skin, I immediately complied, excited I got to hold my baby again!! My hubby is frustrated and says "I'm the dad I could have done that, I have been here the whole time with him!" the nurse replies "You not mom!" He huffed and I remember that he hadn't been able to hold him the whole time he was sitting up here with him.

We laugh about it now but at the time I remember the hurt in my hubby's eyes, he loves he boys with everything he has. The nurse quickly added, "Baby knows mom's heartbeat, is why we say mom needs to do this." I sit down and they hand me Matthew, I'm terrified, he is so small and there are so many cords and wires and beeping machines hooked up to this tiny lil angel.

I remember holding him and feeling so much love and so very scared of losing him all at the same time. It is truly horrifying to see your baby or child hooked up to so many machines to keep them alive. As I held Matthew to my chest his heart rhythm seemed to match up to mine and he never stopped breathing again after that!

It was like magic. The nurse had been 100% right, mom needs baby as much as baby needs mom. I remember just holding him, staring at his tiny lil self, so thankful he was ok and alive and just terrified for him all at the same time.

Soon we realized my incision was not doing well and it started to separate and go with infection. We had a nurse look at it and she then had a Doctor look at it and the Doctor let me know if it continued I would soon be admitted to the hospital as well. For now they gave me antibiotics.

Monday December 25th 2017 arrived and my hubby and I were still at the hospital in Eugene while my parents had my now one year lil boy we back home in Roseburg. I was missing his first birthday and Christmas because I couldn't leave the hospital, emotionally or physically.

I knew if I pushed it and went home for the day it could possibly rip me open more and at the physical state I was in the Doctor strongly advised against it. And in the end we stayed up at the hospital and had cafeteria Christmas dinner together, which was one of the most relaxing holidays I've ever had. My parents sent pictures of my lil man opening gifts and having fun, I cried, I was missing his first birthday and it hit my emotionally ramped up self hard.

My father then surprised me with the best present I had ever had in my life. He drove the hour up to Eugene so I could see my son on his birthday and Christmas. To me there was no greater gift than that, my heart was so full of love I cried and couldn't even get a thank you out of my mouth through the tears of joy. My fathers wet eyes and smile told me he knew what he had done for me that day.

8

Chapter 8

The next day my hubby prepared to go home and back to work, as you all know everyone has bills to pay. So Tuesday the 26th in the afternoon he drove the hour home and I was alone in the hospital with my baby. My sister who was living in Mt Angel at the time drove the hour and a half down to sit with me in the hospital and visit for a few hours. I was thankful to see her and be able to visit in this trying time, I wish she could have stayed the rest of the time with me.

For the next nine days, I sat in the hospital healing and holding my baby. When Matthew was able to drink a whole bottle they would remove the feeding tube from him, as the days passed I watched as they slowly removed one cord after another until finally the time came when he only had his heart rate monitor left.

After a total of 15 days in the hospital lil Matthew and I were able to finally go home, my hubby picked us up and drove us home. I was so very excited to go home and to finally be out of the hospital. To be able to love and care for my son the way I wanted to. To be able to bring lil william home to meet his new baby brother, to show Matthew his new home.

Over the next few weeks life was insane. My hubby worked full time and more to make our ends meet since we were now a one income family now. My mother took over my job at the family business as I was now a full time mom of our Irish twins. And my mother n law worked full time and had neck and back issues which made it impossible for her to lift the boys or watch them. My sister lived three hours away to the north, so we didn't have much family help.

So here I am alone in a half tore up house with a half tore up body, living out of a microwave and fridge to heat bottles and food, while my hubby worked 16 hour days. Very soon postpartum reared its ugly head. My euphoria of being a new mom soon faded and the struggle of taking care of a one year old and a newborn with a double back to back cesarean was beginning to take its toll on me.

The depression became intense and scary, I was upset and unbelievably sad, I started wishing for my old life before kids and a half torn up house. When I actually got to see and spend time with my husband. It's hard to even write about how I was feeling during this time in my life, it's like a dark shadow spreads over your sunny world and suddenly all the things that should bring you joy bring you sorrow.

I remember being so tired, I would cry when I would hear one of the boys wake up crying. I just wanted some sleep, some peace and quiet. I remember falling even deeper and started thinking they would be better off without me. That I was just going to bring them down, that I was a bad mother for ever thinking any dark thoughts of ending it. I was so, so tired, but so was my husband. He worked non stop to make ends meet, he never got to do anything he wanted to. He envied me for being home thinking I was able to do what I pleased and I envied the fact that he could get away from home, from the boys.

These weeks were by far the hardest, my heart broke for feeling this way. I soon contacted my OBGYN and she prescribed me something to help. At first I was embarrassed to make the call, but so thankful I did. I can't imagine being stuck in that state of mind longer than I had been.

Maybe if moms knew it was okay to get help from a Doctor there would be less incidents with moms, babies and children. If you need help get help. If you are hurting inside let your Doctor know.

Soon after my consultation with my Doctor and a prescription, life returned to normal, well as normal as it could be at the time. My life was literally to wake to the sound of crying every few hours, feed, burp, change diapers, rock back to sleep, except now I no longer wanted to cry all the time.

It's amazing how time turns into this crazy blur of auto pilot. I was lucky some days if I was able to brush my hair or teeth. I remember my husband one night asking me why I didn't wear makeup ever anymore, I responded with "I didn't get a chance to brush my hair today lil alone put on makeup."

He had absolutely no idea what life was like with two babies non stop with no breaks, no family support and he had to work constantly to afford for me to be home with the boys. We were willing to do anything to keep the boys out of daycare, though because we had heard enough horror stories to make us terrified by the idea.

He was worn out from work non stop, I was worn out from non stop baby madness. Going from a two income family to a one income family with debt and a new mortgage and two babies, we had to make some serious life changes to keep me at home with the boys. We started off by selling our expansive newer nicer vehicles for older ones we did not have payments on.

Then we consolidated our debt which is something I have done a few times in the past however I never seemed to learn to cancel the credit cards, in doing so we paid things off into a nice lil consolidation loan. Paid cash for William's truck bought from a friend, and I found a lil Dodge nitro for cheap. However we ended up back in the same pot many times over with our debt, credit cards, and instant gratification are a sure way to end up in nothing but debt. But together we managed to make it work, one day at a time.

9

Conclusion

In the last 6 years of being a mom, and five years of being a stay at home mom to Irish twin boys, I have learned to roll with the punches, that nothing is permanent and everything changes.

Time is a blur of tears, laughter, love and heartache. There are moments you will remember forever etched into your mind like a tattoo, then there are the moments that are so fleeting they just pass you by. Sitting here I started this book and was headed in a different direction, now after reflecting on the most memorable times in my life, my book has ended up here with a completely different story from the one I had intended to write.

Looking back at all the impossible struggles, the fights between my husband and I over making ends meet or how we wanted our boys to be raised. All the tears and moments when I felt like I was going to break, that I could not do this, be a wife and a mother and somehow still be me? However I realize now I did end up finding myself, as a mother and as a wife.

I owe my husband the world for working as hard as he had to, to make ends meet while I stayed home and got to be a mom to our boys. Some days were so impossibly hard and frustrating, but looking back now I wouldn't have changed a thing!

Thank you my love for being there for me every step of the way!